THE BOOK OF
JOB

ONE MAN'S JOURNEY TO STAND FOR GOD

VAN ROGERS

RED PRESS CO.
redpressco.com

This is a work protected under the First Ammendment to the
Constitution, as an opinion. Quoted Bible verses are from the
King James edition.

Ordering Information:
Quantity sales. Special discounts are available on quantity pur-
chases by corporations, associations, and others. For details,
contact published@redpressco.com

Cover Photo by Ian Froome, view from Manhattan

ISBN 978-1-7320639-1-4

LCCN 2018938182

Contents

The Land of Uz 1

The Adversary 8

The Contract 12

The Holy Spirit 23

My Testimony 27

Me and My Becoming Job 41

Facts & Observations 65

Prayers That Will Work For You 82

The Wedding... 84

The Church and The Prophets 87

Love 92

Me Personally 94

For Tom, my mentor

FOREWARD

God is love. Everything that he does is out of love. He is not mad at anybody. He does not carry grudges. He had a brilliant plan. Create all the children at one time. Spend billions of years getting to know each child personally. Tell each child about His plan for their life on earth. They all approve of what He asks them to do or go through, then take away those memories before it is our turn to come to earth. He places each of us on earth, at the proper time and gives us free will, once we are here. He lets us individually place ourselves, where we belong in His family. This book will give you the chance to improve your life. God will have His family. I love my God and with all my heart, mind, body, soul and strength.

- Van Rogers

CHAPTER ONE

The Land of Uz

The Lord has never given anyone the true interpretation of the book of Job. It is the one place to get an accurate picture of the relationship between Satan and God. It takes two things to truly understand exactly where we stand in history today. Number one is the true understanding of the book of Job, and the second is the understanding of how this works perfectly to explain Daniel 7:25-26.

The book of Job sticks out like a sore thumb. The length of Job's life alone dictates that this book should have been placed in the book of Genesis. Job 42:16 "After this lived Job a hundred and forty years." God has never made a mistake. By putting Job out of chronological order, God has put to folly the prophets that are trying to interpret the end times.

Job was an intercessor for the Land of Uz. Job was not judged instead of Uz. Job went through his trials and did not sin. This allowed the judgment of Uz at that time to be postponed for one hundred and forty years, which was four generations at that time.

This book will explain to you that Job was actually the First of Six events between God and Satan concerning mankind. Satan approached God and told him that he felt that he was worthy to be treated as a God himself.

> *"I will ascend above the heights of the clouds; I will be like the Most High." - Isaiah 14:14*

> *"And he shall speak great words against the Most High." - Daniel 7:25*

I asked the Lord one day, "How smart is Satan?"

He replied, "One million times smarter than you are."

Then I asked, "How much smarter are you than Satan is?"

He replied, "One trillion times one trillion at least."

Those numbers are true, and that is why no man can truly understand the wisdom of God.

We need to understand what God was thinking at the very beginning of time. There he was with Himself, Jesus, and the Holy Spirit. That in today's language is, Me, Myself, and I. His true hunger was love its self. To feel love, to give love. God came up with the perfect plan. An entire family developed from free will. Every single person will place themselves in God's family.

In order to have free will, every person must have a choice. Satan had to exist, and his decision had to come through his own free will. God saw that if he made Satan smart enough that he would rebel in his own time. In due time, Satan did rebel and talked one-third of the angels into following him.

Read Job 1-2:10 several times. Look at the two encounters that God had with Satan. During the second encounter in Job 2:1, It says that Satan came also among them to present himself before the Lord. Not one time in either encounter did God's or Satan's actions differ from what you would expect to see in a court of law.

After the presidential election last year, God had me to watch the U.S. Senate a lot, usually three times a day. This went on for months. This summer, God finally said, "That is my exact relationship with Satan." It is easy for me to understand now why things in the spirit world are so legal. The Senate is not fun to watch as a Christian. It is the refined, diplomatic version of good versus evil. Pro-life, law and order versus abortion, people's rights, and hate. Rules of behavior apply, just like in Job.

Satan is well described in Isaiah 14:12-16, and in Ezekiel 28:2-19. Satan knew enough about God to know that his only path to success was to confront God about his desires. We need to remember that God had to have this confrontation in order to have free will. Satan wanted both angels and men to worship him alone as their God. God described the "Lake of Fire" to Satan. God told Satan that if they could agree on six events to be challenged, that there could be a legal contract drawn between them. God told Satan that if He (God) won, that He would require Satan to allow himself to be cast into the "Lake of Fire."

The six events in order of happening are:

1. Job living through his trials without cursing God.
2. Moses delivering God's children from Egypt and getting across the Red Sea.
3. God himself coming as a mortal man and finishing his ministry.
4. Israel once again becoming a nation.
5. Another man to be tried by Satan. A man who must endure without sinning, to postpone a deserved judgment for another four generations.
6. If Satan has failed in the first five events, then he has one thousand years in hell to convince just one man to follow him to deceive the nations.

Jesus has unlimited power to show any person or spirit anything that He chooses to do. In John 21:25, John said that if all the things that Jesus did were written down in books, the world itself could not contain them.

Remember that Satan is one million times smarter than we are. God showed Satan the Future. Satan's negotiating skills are second only to God's. Satan was putting his very existence in jeopardy.

Satan did not accept this challenge immediately. There were long negotiations between two terrific lawyers.

What God Offered Satan:

    a. Control of the whole world

    b. His preachers (saints) and prophets to preach the judgment at the wrong time

    c. His Sabbath day

    d. His laws

Things Satan negotiated for and got:

    a. "Sin Nature" starting with Adam and Eve

    b. For the firstborn of the "seed" from God's created couple to be the "seed" for his Kingdom

    c. Language put in God's scriptures (Bible) proclaiming that he has children that belong to him

    d. Church to be broken into fragments which do not pray together

    e. God's preachers (saints) to preach these things with "passion"

The Contract is formed.

The Contract

(As show to me by God)

One Clear Winner
Six events to be challenged by Satan (Page 4)

For the Winner:

Satan
1. Gets recognized by God as an equal to Himself
2. No Lake of Fire
3. Forever right to go anywhere that he chooses in everything that God creates
4. Owns every man who went to hell

God
1. Satan in Lake of Fire

Advantages given Satan:
Nine things from the previous page

Advantage God: Love

Brain Power
Mankind=1
Satan=1,000,000
God=1,000,000,000,000,000,000,000,000,000,000

The Land of Uz was very much like the United States is today. In Job 42:8, the Lord told the friends of Job to take seven bullocks and seven rams and go to my servant Job, and offer up for yourselves a burnt offering; and my servant Job shall pray for you: for him will I accept. In verse Job 42:11, it says that every man also gave him a piece of money, and every one an earring of gold. The livestock, money, and the gold earrings all represent a people of wealth, much like the U.S. is today.

The one other thing that stands out is a snapshot of the near future. God's children will be praying for those who are not. The ones who are not will share their wealth with those children who are accepted by God.

> *"And all the mingled people, and all the Kings of the land of Uz."* - *Jeremiah 25:20.*

Many kings and a wealthy people.

> *21 "Rejoice and be glad O daughter of Edom, that dwellest in the Land of Uz; the cup also shall pass through unto thee: thou shalt be drunken, and shalt make thyself naked. 22 The punishment of thine iniquity is accomplished, O daughter of Zion; he will no more carry thee away into captivity: he will visit thine iniquity, O daughter of Edom; he will discover thy "sins."* - *Lamentations 4:21-22*

The Land of Uz was judged after four generations, likely destroyed because experts today do not even know its location.

CHAPTER TWO

The Adversary

At the first of this book, I explained to you about the need to build a foundation of understanding regarding the relationship, between Satan and God, and the true purpose of the book of Job. As you read this book, you will read my testimony and my story about the last twelve years of my life. They are true and will stand the scrutiny that men will apply. The things that I have written and the rest of this book have come by one method. That method is "saith the Lord."

Adam was created by God; Eve was created from one of Adam's ribs. Every man born since then is a direct descendant of them. God had given Adam dominion over the whole world. It does not matter that Eve fell first. They fell together as a couple. Dominion over the whole earth was given to Satan. That was one of the nine advantages that God gave to Satan in their contract. Just exactly like buying a suit of clothes, Adam and Eve put on the "sin nature" and were forced to leave the garden of Eden. Every person born since then has had to wear the "sin nature," like an invisible suit of clothes. When one of the great television preachers talks about his youth, he says it this way, "If you were not having fun when you were sinning, you were doing it wrong." The "sin nature" is the second of nine advantages given to Satan.

The third thing that Satan received was the "firstborn" from God's created couple. Think about the significance that God placed on the "firstborn." God had to give Cain to Satan as part of their contract.

> *"And now thou art cursed from the earth, which hath opened her mouth to receive thy brothers blood from thy hand." - Genesis 4:11*

God had given what would have been his "first fruit" to Satan for his "first seed."

The fourth thing that Satan got was to put enough of his language into the scriptures and the Bible to accomplish two things. Number one is to show ownership of his children (seed). Number two is the language to separate the Church into separate denominations, each bound in their lies.

> *"Certain men, the children of Belial are gone from among you, and have withdrawn the inhabitants of their city, saying, let us go and serve other gods, which ye have not known." - Deuteronomy 13:13*

> *"... behold, the men of the city, certain sons of Belial" - Judges 19:22*

> *"let not my Lord, I pray thee, regard this man of Belial, even Nabal." - 1 Samuel 25:25*

"Jesus answered them, 'Have not I chosen you twelve, and one of you is a devil?'" - John 6:70

"But the fearful, and unbelieving, and the abominable, and murders, and whoremongers, and sorcerers, and idolaters, and all liars shall have their part in the lake which burneth with fire and brimstone: which is the second death." - Revelation 21:8

I have heard a lot of preachers say, "A tree must lay where it has fallen."

This language was put in the Bible for one reason. To get Satan to agree to the contract and put his soul, on the line.

"God forbid: Yea, let God be true, but every man a liar; as it is written." - Romans 3:4

All men would be condemned according to scripture.

Every man born of Adam and Eve belongs to God, and each has his own place in God's family.

"The Lord is longsuffering to us-ward, not willing that any should perish, but that all should come to repentance." - 2 Peter 3:9

"Who will have all men to be saved and to come into the knowledge of the truth." - 1 Timothy 2:4

"For it is written, as I live, saith the Lord, every knee shall bow to me, and every tongue shall confess to God" - Romans 14:11

This is repeated in Philippians 2:10-11. If any man truly belonged to Satan, then God would not have the authority to tell him what to do. King David is guilty of adultery and first-degree murder. We need to leave judging people up to God.

I have given you the knowledge that is needed to understand the book of Job. Combine that with the correct understanding of God's relationship with Satan.

CHAPTER THREE

The Contract

This summer the Lord told me to get my Bible, and he would show me where we are at today, He said to turn to Daniel 7:25-26.

25 And he shall speak great words against the most High, and shall wear out the saints of the most High, and think to change times and laws: and they shall be given into his hand until a time and times and the dividing of time.

26 But the judgment shall sit, and they shall take away his dominion, to consume and to destroy it unto the end.

God said that when Jesus lived, He had brought the time of grace to the world. He said that when Jesus speaks this phrase, "My family is finished," that the period of "grace" will be ended. The millennium will begin at that second. That single second is the dividing of time. Today, we are in the times before the dividing of time.

This knowledge can now be used to help us understand Daniel 7:25-26.

"...and shall wear out the saints of the most High." Daniel 7:25 is a very accurate description of this part of the contract." Verse 25, "and think to change times and laws: and they shall be given into his hand until a time and times and the dividing of time." This is the legal language of the "contract."

Verse 26 "But the judgment shall sit, and they shall take away his dominion, to consume and to destroy it unto the end." This verse leaves no doubt that the judgment comes after Satan is exposed and confined to hell. God's judgment is going to happen at the proper time, but this is not the proper time. Ninety-five percent of the preachers and prophets are preaching judgment, now, because it was agreed to in the "contract" by God.

Satan was able to change times by changing the day of Sabbath. God's laws are stated in Deuteronomy 28. God's laws guaranteed any person that obeyed him, health and prosperity. This perfect hedge is clearly defined in Job 1:10

> *"Hast not thou made a hedge about him, and about his house, and about all that he hath on every side: Thou has blessed the work of his hands, and his substance is increased in the Land."*

> *"And the Lord said unto Satan, Behold, all that he hath is in thy power." - Job 1:12*

God transferred his laws into Satan's hand right there.

> *"although thou movedst me against him, to destroy him without cause." - Job 2:3*

Job never lied.

"For he breaketh me with a tempest, and multiplieth my wounds without cause." - Job 9:17

God did not explain the purpose of Job's trials to him. Job had no idea that he was the first event in the "contract" between Satan and God. Job only knew that he had done nothing to break God's laws. Even today there are millions of people that love the Lord. They have followed his laws, but they are sick or poor or both.

Twelve years ago, the Lord called my name. I thought for sure that I was going to be a preacher. I had thirteen Christian channels that I really liked to watch on television. The seventh day Adventists had some terrific preachers on their channel. Sometimes I would have to change away from their channel because they would start to say bad things about the Catholic church.

Part of growing up as a Methodist was reading the Apostle's Creed every Sunday. One line that I remember was: "God bless the Holy Catholic Church." I started to turn the channel one day, and the Lord said "I want you to watch this."

"And the ten horns out of this Kingdom are ten kings that shall arise: and another shall arise after them, and he shall be diverse from the first, and he shall subdue three Kings." - Daniel 7:24

That preacher said that in the 300 's AD, there were ten Kingdoms on earth at that time. The Catholic Church declared that it not only wanted to be a church but that it wanted to rule as well. Three of the existing Kingdoms said absolutely no. Satan was the head of the church, and the army of Rome was his weapon. It took two hundred years for the Roman army to complete the destruction of those three Kingdoms. That preacher on television was standing in front of a very small structure, which had been used as a temple. He said that temple was the only structure left out of the entire three Kingdoms.

The other seven kingdoms surrendered without a fight. During that two hundred years is when the Catholic Church changed the day of Sabbath. Saturday is the correct Sabbath day, but God had given his Sabbath to Satan in the "contract." The preacher said the Catholics began to rule in 558 AD. The church led such a slaughter of people that it is known as the "dark ages." Five hundred million people were killed in the name of God. That preacher said that in 1798 AD, Napoleon defeated Rome and put the Pope in prison. He said that twelve-hundred-and-forty-year period had fulfilled another of Daniel's prophecies.

The preacher had copies of pages from the Catholic doctrines. According to those pages, they believe that God has gone from the earth. They believe that God has anointed the Pope to act on his behalf until he returns. Their doctrine was very simple; if you disagreed with us, we have the right to kill you. They showed these pages of their doctrines on television.

During the sixteen hundreds, King James was given an unction by God. He was to have the scriptures translated into English. The Catholics decided to let other churches be formed.

The Catholics paid a man named Francisco Ribera, to write the "Rapture theory." Every church that was formed had to come before the Catholics, for their approval. Every person or group that felt different had to have permission from the Catholics. Every denomination had to agree on how it was different, what, and how to preach. Every church had to preach the "Rapture now theory." The threat of death to the preachers and their families was very real. This is exactly how Satan was able to split the church into all denominations.

That first program that God told me to watch turned into three consecutive programs. The facts that I just shared with you came from those three programs. Those Seventh-Day preachers did not know what was wrong with the "rapture theory." They only knew that Satan had it written and therefore something had to be wrong with it. This splitting of the church was included in the "contract" between God and Satan.

I met a group of people who were being led by a retired Seventh-Day Adventist preacher at his home. That man had the entire Bible memorized. I spent an entire Saturday at his home. They sang songs until breaking for lunch. The ladies fed us and washed the dishes. About one-thirty, we gathered around the table with our Bibles. Each person took his turn reading scriptures. Then the group would discuss what had been read. Everything led by the older preacher.

I left that night about 8 o'clock. The group was still going strong. I thought that it had been the best experience of my spiritual life. The preacher followed me to my truck and asked if I had plans to come back. I told him that it had been a great day and that I was certainly going to pray about it. He said to me, "Van, you cannot go back now. You know the truth about Saturday Sabbath. If you go back now, you will be breaking one of the Ten Commandments. You will be in danger of going to hell." That threw water on what had been a great day. I never went back. I also learned later that they would have asked me to renounce "speaking in tongues." A gift that the Lord had given me two years earlier. Saturday Sabbath is correct, and it is great, but it was given to Satan in the "contract."

Sunday Sabbath is great, and it is fine with God. There will be a time very soon that there will be a need to have two days of Sabbath. I was watching a panel of Seventh-day preachers on television. They said that when a lady named Ellen G. White was leading their church, that they were almost able to call Jesus back to earth. They believe that it's their faithfulness to Saturday Sabbath which gives only their church the authority to call Jesus back to earth.

No man or church is able to call Jesus back. Jesus is not coming back to the Earth until the time of the judgment. Our churches are full of beautiful, wonderful people who love the Lord.

But every denomination has been bound into false beliefs by Satan. I identified three problems in the Seventh-day church. This is the time in history that God is going to break those bonds away from each church. The reason that it is important to talk about each problem with each church is critical. Satan and God have a legal dispute. Each denomination has to be prayed for separately.

About ten years ago I was still in bed early one morning. I was asking God to arm me with any tool or gift that

I would need to work with. I was thinking of wisdom and energy; but instead, the Lord gave me the gift of tongues. To suddenly realize that something inside of me was alive, and it was talking. I had no control of the spirit that was talking or understanding of the words that it was speaking. I was a grown man, but honestly, it scared me. I jumped out of bed, took a shower and went to find some answers. My sister and her husband Tom had experienced miracles. I knew that they would have an answer for me. I went into their house and shared with them what had happened to me. I remember saying to them. There is something inside of me. This thing is alive, and it is talking. I said that if this thing was from God, that I would learn to deal with it. I said that if this thing was not from God, that I was in need of an exorcism, right now.

Tom said, "Let me get a pencil and paper and I will interpret." The spirit spoke again, and there was a very good interpretation.

I will not say that everyone is supposed to speak in tongues. I will say that this gift is priceless to me. I can say without a doubt that what holds most people back, is the beliefs of the churches they attend. I grew up in a Methodist church that my grandfather had helped build. My mother had taught a Sunday school class there for thirty-five years. She had passed on, but that was the only church that I knew anything about. I thought that they would be elated for me. I had no idea that our church does not believe in this gift. I was rejected without being told why. I was treated like I had the flu. About a year and a half of rejection was all that I could stand. It was time to move to another church.

A man talked me into giving his church a try. That church was Baptist; their preacher is a strong man of God. I really liked that church. I waited almost two years before I talked with the preacher about my gift of tongues.

> *"But when that which is perfect is come, then that which is in part shall be done away." - 1 Corinthians 13:10*

He said that the Bible is perfect and therefore tongues are a dead gift. He said that if I would renounce my gift of tongues, that I would be welcome at his church. I told him that no one was going to convince me that God had given me a dead gift.

I really did like that church. It hurt my feelings when I was pushed into leaving. I asked God if he would talk to me about that and he said that he would. These are the things that he either said or showed me.

We, humans, are too loose with our words. Two words that are terribly misused are love and perfect. Love should be reserved for God, things of God, and his children. I love my car. I love my boat. I love my dog. I love football. I love my clothes. I love chocolate. I love ice cream. I love food. I have been guilty of saying several of those myself. God, Jesus and the Holy Spirit are the only things on the face of the earth which have ever been perfect. The Catholics mandated that all churches would preach that the Bible is perfect. They did that for two major reasons. The first is to establish as a fact that Satan has sons that belong to him. That is a lie. The second is to stop the use of tongues in church. What the Bible actually says in Revelations 22:18-

19, is that if you add to or subtract from the scriptures; that you will bring curses down on your own head. My King James Bible is the only book that I have read in the last ten years. It is of God, and I love it. The Bible is perfectly written just as God wanted it to be. The Bible itself is not God, and therefore it is not perfect.

These are also some of the things God has shown me. "

> *If any man come to me and hate not his father and mother and wife, and children and brethren and sisters, yea and his own life, also he cannot be my disciple." - Luke 14:26*

God never spoke of hate concerning our family. The word "hate" should have be translated, "Love them less."

> *"And call no man your father upon the earth; for one is your Father which is in heaven." - Matthew 23:9*

The first father should have been translated "Creator."

In 2nd Chronicles 21, the story of a very bad king named Jehoram is told. In verse 16, the Lord stirred up the Philistines and the Arabians to attack and carry away his household. In verse 17, it says that only his youngest son "Jehoahaz" was left. In verse 20 the Bible says that Jehoram was thirty-two years old when he began to reign. He reigned eight years and died. In 22:1 the Bible says that the inhabitants of Jerusalem made "Ahaziah" his youngest son to reign in his stead. In verse 2 it says that Ahaziah was forty-two years old when he began to reign. In seven verses from 2 Chronicles 21:16 to 2nd Chronicles 22:2, we learned that Jehoram had two youngest sons, "Jehoahaz, and "Ahaziah."

We learned that his youngest son, Ahaziah, was two years older than his father Jehoram when he began to reign.

I am a father. You cannot have two youngest children. Your youngest child cannot be older than you are.

The Lord wanted me to talk about one more point now: the disdain that the apostle Paul had for women.

> *"And Adam was not deceived, but the woman being deceived was in the transgression." - 1 Timothy 2:14*

God is in the process of growing himself a family to share his love with. God saw that Adam was not complete without a mate. He took a rib from Adam and made Eve for him. Adam said, 'This is now bone of my bones, and flesh of my flesh." He said, "a man shall leave his father and his mother and shall cleave unto his wife: and they shall be one flesh." In 1st Timothy 2: 10-14, Paul gives the women a hard time, encouraging silence. In 1st Corinthians 7:1-9, Paul goes too far with his language. He said that it is good for a man not to touch a woman. In verse 6 he said, "But I speak this by permission, and not of commandment." The Baptists will not allow women to preach because of these teachings. Anyone who has heard Joyce Meyer, Paula White, or Beth Moore preach, know that Paul was wrong in trying to exclude women from the ministry.

God is the Creator. He alone decides the order of things

> *"And the Lord said unto Moses, See, I have made thee a god to Pharaoh." - Exodus 7:1*

In the "contract" with Satan, God gave the whole world to Satan. In 2 Corinthians 4:4, Paul was referring to Satan when he said "...the god of this world."

We need to go back to the six events. Job endured his trials without sinning to postpone that judgment for four generations.

Satan had Moses trapped at the shore of the Red Sea. God performed a miracle and gave them dry passage to safety. Pharaoh, however, got his whole army destroyed, trying to catch them.

Herod the King had all the male children under two years old killed, but missed baby Jesus. The ministry of Jesus was short but powerful beyond words. Before he died on the cross, he said, "It is finished." He was referring to his event in the "contract" with Satan.

In 1948, Israel was again given the Land by the UN, to become a nation. Six Arab nations walked out in protest. Nobody but God could have gotten the nations to vote in favor of Israel.

This brings us to the fifth event, and that is me. The Lord wants me to talk to you about some other things before that.

CHAPTER FOUR

The Holy Spirit

T he understanding of the book you are now reading is the gasoline and the matches to burn the
glory from Satan before he is confined to hell.
God called me into his service twelve years ago. The last
eleven years have been the most intense experience of
my life. In Ephesians 6:12, Paul said: "For we wrestle not
against flesh and blood, but against principalities, against
the rulers of the darkness of this world, against spiritual
wickedness in high places." Paul said to wear the armor
of the Christian; truth, righteousness, peace, faith, and sal-
vation." The sword of the spirit has two meanings. One
meaning is knowledge of the Bible, being able to quote
the Bible, Eph. 6:17. The second meaning is to speak in
tongues.

The Lord said that I should write some more facts about
this gift. The Lord had allowed me to become charismatic.
The ability to speak in tongues anytime that I wanted to,
for a purpose. I enjoyed the gift, and I did it often. There
was a small wart that had grown on my shoulder. I spoke
against the wart every morning when I shaved. About two
months later, I visited a church where everyone spoke in

tongues. The preacher told everyone to rise and speak in tongues, and they did. His wife was loud and looked like a cheerleader. I had been given the gift of interpretation, but I did not understand a single word spoken by anyone.

When I got home, I asked the Lord what was said at church.

He replied, "One person said the grass is green. Another person said my favorite color is yellow."

I said, "Father, what have I been saying to the wart?"

He replied, "Mostly about the weather."

Think about it. Telling the Holy Spirit to speak anytime you choose is a dumb idea. That is like telling your dog to speak and hearing him bark. God has twice as many spirits as Satan does, but only he has the true power and authority of God. A short time later, I prayed this: "Father, I love to hear you speak, but I have no desire to hear any other spirit speak. Father when you give me the unction to speak in tongues; Let it always be you and let it always bring glory to your Kingdom."

I burned the wart with a match, three days in a row. It fell off in about two weeks.

I am identifying many of the lies that Satan has our churches bound in. When that is done, there will be the greatest revival that this world has ever seen, it is the great harvest; it is the marriage supper of the Lamb. God will have people in every single church that he has prepared and empowered by the Holy Spirit to handle the "spirits." If you are one of the people in your church that God wants to deal with these spirits, you need to understand this: The Holy Spirit lives in you. He is neither deaf nor dumb. He knows each of the "spirits" by their own name. He has the ability to hurt them. He is an offensive weapon against them.

I was at the house of a friend. He had the spirit of fear on him. God spoke in tongues with the man, before I left his house. As I drove away from the house, I asked Father if he had taken that spirit from the man. He said that he did. Father had me to pull over into a wide place on the shoulder of the road. I stopped, and Father spoke in tongues again. I asked Father what he had said. He said that spirit had stepped into his own snare. He will feel fear for the rest of his existence.

> *"Let the wicked fall into their own nets, whilst that I withal escape." - Psalm 141:10*

That was the first time that I had seen the Holy Spirit be an offensive weapon.

Read Job 1:1 through 2:10. The spirits on both sides can do no more to you than God allows. The worst danger to you will be if you refuse to be used by Him.

About seven years ago, I and some men had logged a job over in Newport, Tennessee. One man had stayed there when I left. About three years ago, he called and asked if I might have a place for him to work. He had an old pickup truck, and after a while, it just died.

It was not worth fixing, and we went to look for him a truck. It took most of the day to find him an affordable truck. While we were riding he said, I believe I have something that I need to tell you about. He said that he and his wife were sleeping one night. In the middle of the night, a spirit came into their bedroom. It grabbed him by his lower leg and lifted him straight up. This man weighs almost three hundred pounds. He said that one shoulder and the top of his head were the only parts of his body that were still touching the mattress. His wife woke up and started to pray for him. It finally left. He said, "Van, that thing squeezed my leg hard enough that it left his handprint bruised into my leg." He said that thing's handprint went from his ankle to his knee. He said that handprint was on his leg for over a month. The Lord has been preparing this man to be used by him ever since we had that talk.

The world is not going to fix itself. Open your heart and do your part for the Lord. You and you alone are responsible for your part. God's plan is perfect, but each of us has a part to do.

Hate comes by people listening to Satan rather than God. Remember the young white man that drove to South Carolina. He killed nine black people while they were in church. There is no doubt that a spirit of hate told that man to do that.

CHAPTER FIVE

My Testimony

During the 1990's I had built a successful logging company. I had twelve separate crews of men who contracted to log for me. I would buy the timber from the landowners. Then I would choose the best crew to use for each job. Most of the jobs required road work to be done. Loaded log trucks weigh up to eighty thousand pounds. Truck roads always improve the value of the property. Each landowner and I would determine where to build the roads, and how far they would extend into their property. Building these roads was the foundation of knowledge that I needed to build a grading company. The grading company was formed in the late 1990's.

Land sales in Western North Carolina were red-hot. These mountains are beautiful, and people came from everywhere to buy or invest. The grading business had grown at a remarkable rate. The company had grown to the point that we were billing our customers about two hundred thousand dollars each week. We kept from four to six jobs going at all times. The customers were wealthy and were making money. It was fun to be involved in those exciting times. A man who lives in the next town had become the "agent" for a family in Europe. He had kept them in his home while they were exchange students as high schoolers. The "agent" and I met, and we came to an agreement to contract their grading work.

Developing property in the mountains is a process. They had built a speculation house. They were asking seven hundred and fifty thousand dollars for it. They had sold several individual lots, but after a while, their payments for our grading work failed to be on time. I called the agent, and he said he had not received the money from Europe. He said that the money would come. I checked my records and saw that the balance that they owed was more than one hundred and fifty thousand dollars. I called the agent back and told him that if they would give me a "second mortgage" against their property, then I could continue working. He agreed, and we signed the legal documents. My other customers were paying on time. I didn't think about it again for a couple more months.

The man from Europe called me one day. He was in a good mood. He said that he had plans to be here in two weeks. He said that he was pleased and that he wanted to pay his debt to me while he was here. That second week was silent. Neither the man from Europe or his "agent" would return my calls. The following week I went to see their lawyer. I asked him if he could legally talk to me about this situation. He said yes that the man from Europe had gone to the bank and bought the "first mortgage." He said that when he had completed that transaction, he had gone back to Europe.

I asked the lawyer if he could tell me what the problem was. He said that the "agent" for the man had taken the money from the individual lot sales. Instead of paying me with the money, he had used it to buy speculation property for himself. I believe that the "agent" thought that his speculation property would sell before anyone found out about it. The man from Europe had grown to love the "agent" when he had lived with him as a teenager. He had felt that I was involved with the "agent" in doing him wrong.

I went to talk to my lawyer about what the man from Europe had done. He said that if the man from Europe had paid off the first mortgage, then my second mortgage would have become the first mortgage. The man from Europe had bought the first mortgage from the bank and therefore became the legal owner of the first mortgage. He said that my second mortgage had the right to buy the first mortgage. My second mortgage would then own the entire property. He said that my second mortgage had no other legal rights. I did not have the necessary money to buy the first mortgage. This was now an uncollectable debt.

We continued to work, but within a few months, the housing market had begun to shut down. Money flow became a difficult problem. I had bought seven and a half million dollars' worth of equipment. I had been able to pay six million dollars from that debt.

That still left me owing a million and a half dollars. I had attached a lot of the equipment that was paid for to the equipment that was not paid for.

Three liens came at one time from different companies. One day a man from Texas called. He said that his company had sold the eleven pieces of equipment which they had re-possessed. The eleven pieces had sold at auction. They had brought four hundred and fifty thousand dollars less than I owed them. He said that he had taken me to court in Texas. He said that the court had found agreement with the action that he had taken against me. He said that was "perfected" judgment. He said that his lawyers were in the process of having this "perfected judgment" transferred to North Carolina. He said that when this process was completed, that he would be able to deal with me through the sheriff's office.

God said, "Tell that man that you will give him fifty thousand dollars to settle the debt, but that you need ninety days to get the money."

I told the man those exact words.

He was quiet for a minute, then he said, "I will call you back tomorrow." The next day he called back. He said, "Van, I am going to take that haircut. However, I am going to fax a document to you right now. This document perfects my lien in North Carolina against you in ninety days."

He sent me the fax, I signed it, and sent it back to him. I went over to my desk and sat down. I leaned back and looked toward heaven. I said, "Father, where do you plan on that money coming from?"

I do not remember having another thought. The telephone rang, and it was my lawyer. He said that he had just gotten off the phone with the lawyer here, who was representing the people from Europe. They had offered one hundred and seventy-five thousand dollars to settle their debt with me.

God said, "Tell him that you want two hundred thousand dollars to settle." I told my lawyer exactly that. I am a grown man, but I shed some tears.

I asked, "Father what do you want me to do now?"

He said to call the other two companies that had sued me. One lawsuit was for two hundred and fifty thousand dollars. The other lawsuit was for one hundred and fifty thousand dollars. God had me to offer the bigger lawsuit, thirty thousand dollars for settlement. He had me offer the smaller lawsuit twenty thousand dollars to settle.

These are corporations and their legal counsel. They have stockholders that they owe a responsibility. No one person is going to take the responsibility of accepting a small offer. The only safety that anyone would have is accepting an offer agreed upon from a board meeting. There were several discussions and counter-offers. God had me to hold my ground on my offers.

Those discussions and counter-offers took a long time. Those two companies did not accept my offers until just before the ninety days was up.

The man from Europe, who would not pay me, had gotten sick. He had given his family business in America to his sister. She lived in London. I got to meet her when she personally brought a bank draft to settle her family's debt with me. She said she had gotten feeling in the "pit of her stomach." She needed to come to America and settle the family debt with me. I got her money one week. The ninety days expired the next week.

God had me to put the hundred thousand dollars left over into the business. We were able to finish our existing jobs. That money along with what we were able to collect, lasted for a year. At that time, the bottom fell out completely. There was around seven thousand dollars left in our bank account. Here come the police serving me with three more lawsuits. I did not even open them up.

A month or two went by. My lawyer called one day and said that my wife and I needed to come and see him. She and I went to his office. He said that he had been on the phone with the lawyer of a really large corporation.

My grading company had purchased the materials needed to install a sewer and water system for a large subdivision. There were a combined fifty-five thousand linear feet of the two systems. My wife and I had signed personally for the materials. The company had sued my wife and me for seven hundred and fifty-four thousand dollars. He said they had hired a powerful lawyer and he was an A-hole. They have hired him to destroy you, and you have no way out. He advised us to hire another lawyer to represent us in bankruptcy. He said if we would do that, we could save our vehicles and our household furniture. He gave me a copy of the lawsuit, and we left. My old truck had over three hundred thousand miles on it. My wife's vehicle was older. Our furniture had very little value.

I asked God if he wanted me to declare bankruptcy. He said no.

Within a few weeks, my wife had put me out of the house. We had completed three million dollars of work and received no pay. Five of the men who had worked with me, in grading, were good loggers. We took a job logging over at Newport, Tennessee. That was about ninety miles from Franklin, NC, my home. I had about six thousand dollars in the Franklin bank. I was paying for our motel in Newport with a credit card.

We went to check-in one Monday morning, and the credit card would not work. I had some cash in my pocket, so I paid for the rooms with that. I went back to Franklin to find out what the problem was with my credit card. The teller checked my account. She said the balance was negative seven hundred and forty-eight thousand dollars. I told her that there had not been a mistake made. I understood exactly what the problem was.

I went outside the bank and asked, "Father, what do you want me to do now?"

He said, "Go to Waynesville, NC, and ask your cousin to loan you ten thousand dollars to work with."

I did as he said and got the money. I put it into a bank in Newport, Tennessee. At that point, I knew the lawsuit was approaching. In a few weeks, we finished the logging job. I gave my cousin his money back before his money could be seized also.

A local contractor called and asked about a track hoe. He needed to rent a track hoe that had a sixty-foot reach. I said that I had one and he rented it for two weeks. I had not been served with any additional paperwork. Making any money sounded like a good idea. The two weeks were over, and he met with me on a Wednesday to pay the rent.

He asked me if I might be willing to sell the machine. I did not want to discuss all those legal details. I just said, well, I would like to and left it at that. The very next day, Thursday, I got a phone call. The man said that he had seen the track hoe that I had rented out. He asked me if I would be interested in selling the machine.

God said, "Tell him yes, that you want sixty thousand dollars for it."

I indicated I would sell to which he inquired an amount. I answered, "I want sixty thousand dollars for it."

We talked for a few minutes. He stated his finding of three liens against me at the courthouse.

He said, "If I buy that machine, I would want to re-sell it. I would need to have a clear title within thirty days. Can you do that?"

God said, "Tell him that will not be a problem." So I replied, "Yes sir, I can, that will not be a problem."

The man said that he would buy the machine and wire the money to me the following day, on Friday. I gave him my bank account numbers in Newport, Tennessee.

The next day before five o'clock, God said, "Call the bank and check on the money." When the teller checked, she found that no money had come.

I spent the weekend reading my Bible and talking with the Lord. On Monday morning as I came back to Franklin, the Lord said to "pull over." There is a large area overlooking Franklin. I pulled in and asked God what he wanted me to do.

He said, "Call the bank and ask about the money."

I called the bank and gave the teller my account number. She said that at five o'clock on Friday, there had been a wire transfer for sixty thousand dollars.

I thanked my Father. I asked, "Father, what would you have me do now?"

He said, "Call the lawyer in Raleigh, NC, who is representing the materials against you."

I still had the copy of the lawsuit that my lawyer had given to me. I found the telephone number of the law firm on the first page. I called the number, and a man answered, asking if he could help me. I told him the name of the man that I needed to speak with. The man said, "That is me." I had never had a lawyer answer the company telephone before, or since, that day.

God said, "Tell him that you will give them fifty thousand dollars to settle this case." I said, "Sir, you don't know me. My name is Van Rogers, and I live in Franklin, NC.

He said, "Van, I know exactly who you are."

I told him that I could offer his client fifty thousand dollars to settle their lawsuit against me. He was quiet for a moment. I did not know what to expect, but when he spoke, it was with a happy voice.

He said, "Van, I think that I can sell that idea to my clients." He said that he would contact his clients and call me back."

I said, "Father, you are amazing. What would you have me do now?"

He said, "Call the man back who bought your track hoe. I want you to sell him your four-wheel drive backhoe, for thirty-six thousand dollars."

I found the man's telephone number and called him. He was surprised to hear from me so soon and asked what I wanted. I told him about the backhoe. He said that it would take about four hours for him to get here. He showed up and inspected the machine. He agreed to pay what I had asked for the backhoe. He said that he would wire the money into my account the next day. That finished Monday.

The next morning, I asked God what he would have me do first.

He said, "Go to the courthouse and get the names of the other two law firms.

These two lawsuits were for a combined four hundred thousand dollars. A year earlier it had taken the two companies two and a half months to accept a fifty thousand offer between them. This time God had me to offer each company, ten cents on each dollar of debt.

It took Tuesday and Wednesday to get that done.

On Thursday, the lawyer representing the big case called me back. He said, "Van, can you actually get fifty thousand dollars?"

I said, "Yes sir, I can."

He said that if I was willing to be a witness for them, they could go through my contractor's license to sue the bank in New England that had not funded the job. He said that their client would take my place in the lawsuit against the bank, and I would be their witness. He asked if I would be willing to do that. I told him that I would be happy to do that. He said that they would accept my offer of settlement. He said they would write me a check to cover my time, and travel expenses to come to Raleigh, NC, to be their witness. He said that it would take some time because they had to prepare the complete lawsuit against the bank. They needed for the lawsuit to be complete before they deposed me as their witness. He said that he would call again when they were ready. During the next two weeks, the smaller claims accepted the offers that I had made to them. I received their legal paperwork, accepting my offers upon receipt of payment. Each time, I would drive to Newport, Tennessee and get them a certified check to send by overnight mail.

On Thursday of the third week, the lawyer on the big suit called back. He said that they would be ready to depose me the following Wednesday. He said that it would take the most of a day to complete the process. I would need to drive to Raleigh on Tuesday, and spend the night. They rented me a hotel room that was close to their office. I went to their office on Wednesday morning. Three lawyers had prepared the case. Each attorney took turns asking me questions. We took a break for lunch. It took two or three hours after lunch to complete the questions. I signed my name to make their case complete. I gave them my check for fifty thousand dollars. They gave me a check for my time and expenses. I asked them to take care of their lien against me and the negative balance at the bank in Franklin. They assured me that they would get those things done. That Friday which had been four weeks and one day, God's work was complete. I had told the man, who purchased the track hoe, thirty days would not be a problem. Twenty-nine days later, the liens were gone from the courthouse, and my bank account was back to zero.

God had taken an uncollectable debt and settled three lawsuits. Those lawsuits totaled eight hundred and fifty thousand dollars. He did that in just under ninety days.

He settled those first three lawsuits for a total of one hundred thousand dollars.

This time, God sold a track hoe and a backhoe. He settled three lawsuits that totaled one million one hundred and fifty thousand dollars. He did that amazing work in twenty-nine days, for ninety thousand dollars, and had six thousand dollars left over. No lawyers on my part, just God.

God told me how he had done it. He told me for a purpose.

I knew that someone had hired a private detective. I had found where he had asked questions about me at businesses in town. The Lord had put it in his mind to do a very thorough job. He had not only checked me out, but he had checked out the developer that had hired me. That developer had already tried to sue the bank and failed. When the lawyer looked at the information that his detective had gathered against me, he had concluded 'if Van Rogers had any money, I could build a case for him against the bank.' When I called him that first Monday morning, offering him fifty thousand dollars for a settlement with his client, he realized 'there is the money.' He was able to call the company that had sued me with an option. *I can get you a fifty thousand dollar settlement now, or I can use that money and Van Rogers' contractor's license to build a case against the bank for you. I believe that I can win that case to get the entire amount.*

That is why he had that happy voice when I made him the offer.

God is smart beyond our comprehension. He told me about how he had done his amazing work for a purpose. He was laying a foundation for me to believe him about how things work. When he tells me about his legal arrangement with Satan, I believe him. When he explains to me about Job, I believe him. How could I ever doubt anything that he tells me?

I thoroughly enjoyed spending that weekend with my Father. I love him, and he loves me. He loves you, just as much as he does me. By Monday we were both ready to talk.

I said, "Father, my marriage is in a shamble. Financially I am still ruined. I feel like a glass full of sand. I cannot see a way for my life to be repaired. The things that you did for me are amazing beyond words. I am approaching sixty years old. I cannot see the purpose that you have for my life."

God said, "I have a great purpose for your life. There are many storms that are coming into your life. I have given you a testimony that is a rock for you to stand on through these storms. Satan will attack you and your family. There will be times when you cannot see the meaning or the purpose for your life. There will be some time before you can see that you have a future. I will ask you to do things for me that you will not understand. True love for me is shown by obedience. I have things to share with you about the future because it is the time to do so. I have things to share about the Bible that are in plain sight, that people have not been able to understand. When I have finished telling you anything; I will say 'Saith the Lord!' 'Saith the Lord', must always be heard. If you are told anything, and you do not hear me speak those words, then I expect you to say this.

'Father, would you repeat that again, in the name of Jesus Christ, who lived in the flesh.'"

One hundred percent of what I know and what I believe came by, "Saith the Lord."

The things that the Lord described have all happened in my life. About seven years have passed since the Lord had that "talk" with me. My family and business were destroyed.

I became the Job for today's world.

Fifty-eight million abortions in America alone. Sin, hate, wars, and rumors of wars. Ninety-five percent of prophets and preachers are calling for judgment now.

Judgment is certainly deserved, but this is not the time for it to happen.

"But the judgment shall sit." - Daniel 7:26

CHAPTER SIX

Me and My Becoming Job

I had been out of church for about 14 years. I went by my mom and dad's house one day to visit. Mom asked me if I was ever going to settle down and raise a family. I told her no before I left that day. One thing that I had never liked was the burden of responsibility. I was forty-one years old, and I wanted to be care-free for the rest of my life. That question that she had asked me turned out to be a word from the Lord. Within several weeks, I developed a hunger to get married and have children. I remembered how much fun it had been to grow up in my parent's house. I loved my mom and dad so much. I wanted to have children who felt the same way about me. I told my mom that I wanted to go to church with her. She was glad to hear that news. I went to church with my mother that Sunday. She always sat in the second row back. I sat there with her and cried like a baby for the entire service. There was no shame or guilt. I went to the altar after church. When we left that day, I felt as clean as a newborn baby. I asked my soul-mate to marry me, and we got married. My mom passed away in 1994. My dad passed away in 1996. My wife and I had three baby girls. The Lord blessed our business with prosperity. We went to church on Sunday and paid our tithe to the Lord.

I had been raised in that Methodist Church. I thought God was all about the next life. I had never heard a person say, "God told me."

I had turned fifty-five years old. One Sunday the preacher said, "If you died today, do you know for a fact that you would go to heaven?"

I thought to myself, "how could anyone possibly know for sure if you were bound for heaven?"

Two weeks later, he said, "I know for a fact that there are people here that the Lord wants more from you than you are giving."

He looked around the church and his eyes connected with mine for just a second. That was the smallest of a push, but it was the Lord calling me. Over the course of several months, a hunger for the Lord came upon me. There are no words to describe that, except to say that I was on "fire." I started to read my Bible a lot more. I carried my Bible with me everywhere. I pursued the Lord relentlessly.

It took eight months for the Lord to speak to me finally.

The first thing he said was "What would you do for your family?"

I said, "Lord, you have found my heart. I am all in, my service, devotion to you, even my life if you need that."

I understood his question and had given him my answer.

The second thing that God said to me was something that I did not understand at the time.

He said, "I have seen your way through your troubles."

Our oldest daughter was misbehaving but other than that everything was really good. God was building a foundation of understanding. He was talking about things that would start in a year or two and continue through today. What he says is usually much "deeper" than it appears to be.

I heard Pastor John Hagee one day on television. He was preaching that men will be on different levels in heaven. It made me mad when I first heard him preach that, but it is true. It took God the most of a year to get my mind changed.

I have told you about these things to get you to stop and think. Take all the time that you need to think about your own personal relationship with God. You will be alone when you stand in front of him. There were ten virgins in Matthew 25. Five of them went to look for the "oil" that they were short on. Think about that. A virgin has not done anything wrong. Half of those ten virgins did not get married. More than half of the people who are in church today do not have a proper relationship with God. We are about to have a tremendous revival. According to Matthew 25, only about half of the church will be married. Make sure that you are one of them.

It is very hard to determine whether what the Bible says is either literal or figurative. The dividing of time in Daniel 7:25, is literally the marriage supper of the Lamb. Right now, we get as close to God as our heart will take us. The five virgins were not allowed to come into the wedding in Matthew 25. The door had been closed. God himself closed the door to the ark in the time of Noah.

There will be a time of great tribulation and judgment. That time is more than a thousand years from now. In this time, that is almost now, will happen just as suddenly. The outcomes will be just as final. Jesus will simply say "My family is finished." Whatever level your heart is on at that second, will never change.

There is language in Matthew 24:19 and Luke 21:23. *Woe to the mothers of young children.* Whatever level that her heart is on is the level that she will bind her child to. She loves her baby so much that she would die for it. She is willing to lock her baby and herself in a wrong level because of lack of knowledge.

> *"My people are destroyed for lack of knowledge."* - Hosea 4:6

I asked God to put this in a realistic setting that I could understand.

He said, "Let us say that I choose to give you the Biltmore House in Asheville, NC."

That is the largest home in America. It is attached to at least eight thousand acres. These acres are in farmland, vineyards and forest lands.

He said, "You would have the lifestyle of a son of mine. Think of how many people and how many levels of people that it takes to run that operation. There are many levels for those that will get to know me as their Father. But look at the levels that will only know me as their God."

Those are the walls of his love that are talked about in Revelation 22.

Look out your window at the world today. God will take away those lower levels of poverty. There are as many levels in the millennium as there are in the rest of the world today. That includes the multi-billionaires and even trillionaires.

I simply said, "Father open my heart to you and take me as high as I can get."

As your heart takes you up in levels, remember 1st Thessalonians 5:17, "Pray without ceasing." This means that you will gradually learn to talk to God, more and more.

Amen!

The Lord had called me when I was fifty-five years old. He gave me a lot of "life experiences," that I needed to learn things from. Going through these experiences are usually not much fun.

I prayed, "Father, let me learn from each thing as I go. I do not need that lesson a second time."

One day without any notice, I was physically attacked by a "Spirit." It was just like a wrestling match. Something that I could not see but I could take hold of it. It could certainly take hold of me. It was difficult, but I finally won, and it left me alone.

That happened quite a few times over the next several months. More than once in front of my family. After several months of winning, I ran into a different situation.

I met a "spirit" that completely dominated me. That "spirit" just wore me out. That happened more than once.

They would throw me ten feet or roll me like a ball, totally dominate.

I was at my brother-in-law's house one day when one of those spirits attacked me. I had gotten to the point that I was yelling for help. My brother-in-law Tom came. He started speaking to it in tongues. It left after Tom started speaking to it in tongues. Tom told me that there was a much better way to fight them, than physically.

I said, "I hope the Lord teaches it to me pretty soon because I am really tired of this."

The next attack came about two weeks later. Same results, completely dominated, totally beaten. I was sitting on the ground where that thing had left me.

I remember saying, "Lord, I am fifty-seven years old. What am I supposed to learn from being beaten up by some spirit?"

The Lord replied, "Do you think that you will ever question if these spirits really exist?"

I said, "Father the question of them being real will never cross my mind again."

That was the last hand to hand fight that I have had with a spirit. Not every one of you will have to encounter spirits physically, but some of you will. A working relationship with the Holy Spirit is by far your best answer.

I learned to cut timber as I grew up, working with my dad and uncle. My dad had passed away in 1996. My uncle had carried his timber knowledge into forming a tree removal business. He called me one day and asked if I would help him with a job. He had contracted to remove some large trees that were standing above a nice home. His crew would get the ropes connected high in each tree. I would cut them down as he would pull them with his loader. Things worked well, and by lunch we had all the bad ones cut down. We stopped for lunch and ate our sandwiches.

We went back to work, and I felt fine. The crew had the next tree hooked up, and I got ready to cut it down. I bent over to cut the tree, and I head-butted the tree with my face. I hit that tree hard enough to stun me. I got up and did the same thing again. I could not stand up again from that point in time. I waved to my uncle. I told him that I would be alright, but to give me the time to get out of the way. I crawled far enough to be out of danger from falling trees. It was a beautiful spring day, and I found a sunny, warm place to stop. I rolled over onto my back, and I started talking to the Lord.

I said, "Father, it is such a beautiful day that you have made. This is a beautiful place. If this is the time that you have chosen to bring me home, then I am ready."

In a minute the Lord said, "This is a spiritual attack, just hold on, and you will be fine."

I laid there for a little while. I called my wife to come and get me, and we left. I called my uncle after I had called my wife. I told him that I would be fine, but I was going home. One of my uncle's crew member told several people that I had a heart attack. I was fine by the next day.

I have had several of those types of attacks since then. There is no doubt in my mind that many people have had a spiritual attack. They have given claim to having a heart attack and died.

I have learned to say, "I do not claim this, and I will not give this a name. It does not matter if the symptoms are of the "flu" or a "cold" The symptoms never last longer than one-half the normal time. This will work for you as well.

My brother-in-law, Tom, became my mentor. Mainly then because of his knowledge about the spirits. Things had started to go wrong with my business and with my family life. I went to Tom's house one day to talk about it.

The first thing that Tom would always say is. "God is Love." He had a much better relationship with the Lord than I did. I asked him to pray and ask God what I was doing wrong. God had blessed all that I had, something I had done must be the problem. He called me in a couple of days and said that God had given him an answer. I went to his house, and this is what he told me.

"God said that he was doing a work of love in your life and that it will not be over until you can see the love in what is happening."

I said to myself then, where can I possibly see love in fussing with my family and things failing in the business: I decided to dig in as hard as I could with the Lord and ride through the troubles. The business failed, my family left me about six and a half years ago. I felt exactly like a glass full of sand that could never be put back together again.

That is the time when God performed that last set of miracles to complete my testimony. God and I had our "talk," and I moved into the apartment where I live now.

Think about the first Job. Those first sets of circumstances could easily have taken two years. Satan would have wanted enough time to wear him down. When his friends came, that part of the story probably did not last for more than a month. A month would be a long time to put up with anybody that did not have one kind word to say about you.

Satan is one million times smarter than we are. His negotiating skill is second only to that of God. It makes sense that while negotiating these events with God, that Satan would see the possibility of failure with the first Job. Attacking this family and me is the last event Satan has before he is put into hell for a thousand years. If killing the first Job's children did not work, why would you do it that way again? This time let each of the children be awesome. Then turn them into being so bad that they are a blight on society. This time let Job love his wife more than he has ever loved anyone else. Let her grow to hate him and curse him in public several times. Let Job's wife grow a relationship with another man. Let her demand that Job and their children accept it. Let Job be in poverty. Let those legal storms come upon him.

Let the years of Job's problems be multiplied. That might sound dramatic, but my life has happened exactly that way. It has been nine years since the last time that my soul-mate told me that she loved me.

All three of our children were great kids. Callie is the oldest. She read a thousand books during her fifth grade. Satan attacked her when she started the sixth grade. Callie loved everything and everybody. She was such a joy to be around. She always had such a pretty smile.

Callie is now twenty-five years old. After fourteen years of rebellion and drugs, there are only twisted snags left of the once beautiful smile.

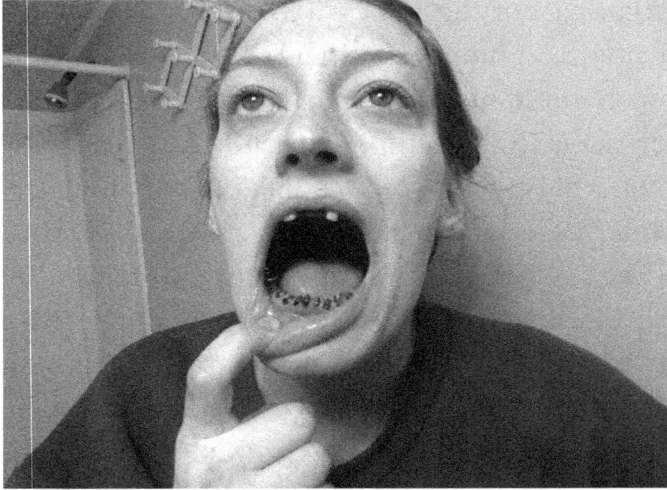

It tears my heart as a parent to watch what Satan did to this family. The two oldest girls have spent a lot of time in jail. My baby girl turns twenty-one next week. She has struggled with both alcohol and drugs.

My soul mate does not know anything about this family being used by God. I know that she wished that she had never met me. I would defend her with anybody. She is only doing what God agreed to with Satan.

I knew that my life was parallel to that of Job. But until God explained things to me this summer, 2017, I could not understand the purpose. I told my kids that I only knew that God had used us for a purpose. I told them that we were "good enough" to be used for God's purpose.

When I moved into this apartment, God spoke to me.

He said, "You need to be more serious about me that you have been."

This is what I had been doing. I carried my Bible everywhere that I went. It had been more than three years since I had read any other book but the Bible. I had thirteen Christian channels on television, and that is what I watched. I had dedicated my life to becoming as close to God, as I could get. How could I possibly do more?

Over the course of the next year, I found out. It is about forty feet from my bed, to my chair in the living room. I spent about half the days that first year without leaving my apartment. I wake up in the morning and talk to Him until he says that it is time to get up. Forty feet to my chair and talk to Him. I would fast until sometime in the afternoon when he tells me that it is time to eat. Ten to fifteen hours a day, read the Bible and talk to God.

There is a lot of time to be quiet and think. That first year, God said several things to make me think more.

One day He said, "I will give you more out of love than the law."

After a time, I came up with this solution. If I close my Bible and look at it as a complete book, then it is the law. If I say, "Father, you said it in the Bible," then I am using the Bible as the law.

God is love. Therefore, I believe that you would rather give me things than to have me ask for things. You will give me what you want to give, in the time that you choose to give it. He said that was the right answer. I have not asked him for anything since that day.

Family

God has a "contract" with Satan. My marriage was to be destroyed. My children would be destroyed. My family was secure financially, that was destroyed. Every decision that I made turned out badly.

One day the Lord said, "I am going to fix your business first, then I'm going to fix your family."

I was very happy with what God had just told me. Every time that the business would need, I would go to the bank and borrow it. My wife would say, "Van, we are secure now. Please think about our children and me." I would always reply, "this is just another test from the Lord, and I will not be found short."

I sold one million four hundred thousand dollars worth of property. I signed liens against the best pieces of property that were left. We had two hundred thousand dollars in our savings account. My wife said, "Van, please don't take that. That money is all the security that we have left." I took the money out and put it into the business.

I did not understand what God had meant when He told me that He was going to "fix" the business, and then He was going to "fix" the family. He meant He was going to put an atomic bomb into each of them, then explode the bombs.

I can almost hear God telling my wife how dumb each of those decisions was. And there were a lot of those dumb decisions. Our lawyer informing us that we were broke and being sued, that was more than she could take. Her love had turned into hate. In April 2018, it will have been seven years since she put me out of her life. It has been over a year since we had our last conversation. There was only one thing that I could say to her at that time. I knew that we, "our family," was good enough in heaven, to be used by God here on earth. That what had happened to us had nothing to do with punishment.

I had a vision that Jesus was holding me, my wife, and our children, by our heels. He was holding us up off the ground, with each hand full. He threw this whole family out into His fire. As any one person would try to crawl out, He would take His foot and push them back in. That is why He told me that when we came out of His "fire" that we would be a strong prayer team for Him.

My wife, and our three girls, all have words from the Lord in their mouths. God said that their "healing anointments" would be "second to none."

Left to Right: Callie, Brittany, Katie, around 2004

Callie, around 2008

Brittany, 2013

In 2017, I have not intruded on my wife at all. I intend to leave her alone and let God finish His work. I expect everyone who knows her and reads this, to do the same.

The Holy Spirit

The Holy Spirit is awesome. He knows all about our relationship with God.

> "But when He, the Spirit of truth, comes, He will guide you into all the truth; for He will not speak on His own initiative, but whatever He hears, He will speak; and He will disclose to you what is to come. 14 He will glorify Me, for He will take of Mine and will disclose it to you. 15 All things that the Father has are Mine; therefore I said that He takes of Mine and will disclose it to you." - John 16:13-15

He helps us know what to say during our prayers. Our prayers flow out of the abundance of our heart. Whenever it is time to pray about anything that has come to my mind. I say, "Father." The Holy Spirit completes the rest of the prayer. I listen to the words that come out to see if there are any directions for me from God.

As the first year went on, God did another thing. God would sometimes add an "R" into "Father." Sometimes when I would start to pray, the first word out would be "Farther." That one was not very hard; it meant not now. Whatever that prayer was about, put it on the "shelf" for now.

I had bought a new set of covers for the bed when I had moved into this apartment. The time came when those sheets needed to be washed. Every time that I would think sheets, the word "Farther "would come out of my mouth. The storms that God told me about had started. I went through several different things with my health. Each time brought heavy sweating at night time. I would sleep in tee shirts during these times. Two hours sleep and you could wring water from the shirt. Wash with a cloth, put on a clean shirt, and do the same thing again.

In the morning, Father would have me "air" out the bed all day and go through the same thing again that night.

God would only say, "Obedience is important."

One time I developed the symptoms of shingles. It was very painful and itched terribly. That lasted more than two months. There were at least four of those heavy sweating periods, that lasted at least two weeks each.

This story needs to come all the way up until now because it is not pleasant to talk about it. At two years of living here, God allowed me to wash the sheets. At the four-year mark, the sheets came into pieces one day. God had me to put new sheets on the bed that day. About seven months ago, God said to turn the sheets around one hundred and eighty degrees. God counts everything. There is always a reason for absolutely everything that he does. In six years the sheets on my bed were washed one time. Replaced new one time, and have been turned once.

The Summer of 2017, God told me that those filthy sheets had represented the sins of the world to him, just as the things that had happened to Job did back then. I was very happy to find out that there was such a good reason for my family and me to endure these trials.

At the end of the first year in the apartment, I came home from church on a Wednesday night.

God said, "I want you to read the Bible." He said, "Go to the book of Ezekiel and read chapter 22." When I finished reading the chapter, he said, "Read verses thirty and thirty-one again.

> *"And I sought for a man among them, that should make up the hedge, and stand in the gap before me for the land, that I should not destroy it: but I found none,"31, "Therefore have I poured out mine indignation upon them; I have consumed them with the fire of my wrath: their own way have I recompensed upon their heads, saith the Lord." - Ezekiel 22:30-31*

I finished reading it the second time.

God said, "Read it again." He had me read those verses six or eight times. Then he was silent.

After several minutes of thinking; I said, "Father, it seems to me that you are asking me a question. You want to know if I am willing to stand in the hedge for you about something. I do not know what I am worthy to stand in the hedge for, but my life is yours to use however you choose to use it."

In a week or two, there came a question about being in solitary. I said that I would not need anything but Him, to be in solitary.

In the middle of the second year here, God said, "You can be more serious than you are now."

> *"For this cause, I Paul, the prisoner of Jesus Christ."*
> *- Ephesians 3:1*

> *"I, therefore, the prisoner of the Lord." - Ephesians 4:1*

> *"Paul, a prisoner of Jesus Christ." - Philemon 1*

That is what God was saying when he talked about "solitary." What God says is often much deeper than it first appears.

In the last five years; there have been about three and a half years that I have sat in my chair all day. I fast, read my Bible, meditate, and watch whatever on television that God wants me to. That means that I will usually fall asleep twice a day in the chair. I have dreams and visions that God talks to me about.

I do not care how comfortable your chair is; your back will hurt, your butt will hurt, your legs and your feet will hurt.

I had to have open heart surgery three years ago. I had not been able to go to the bathroom in three days. I started to have hallucinations during that third day. I called my daughter and asked her to bring me a laxative. I thought that not going to the bathroom was causing my problems. I felt drunk as well as having the hallucinations. I could not drive. My daughter talked my ex-wife into bringing the laxative instead of her.

When she saw me, she said "Van, you are in trouble, you need help."

She drove me to the Franklin hospital. They got me on oxygen and an IV. The ambulance took me to Mission Hospital in Asheville, NC. They took me to the heart unit. The next thing that I remember is looking at a big monitor screen with the doctor.

He said, "Van you have had a heart valve failure."

My heart would beat, and a river of blood would go up. My heart would relax, and the blood would just flow back down. Just like a yo-yo.

He said, "You have a choice to make. I can repair the valve, or you can choose to die. There is no oxygen going to your brain. Your body function cannot work without blood flow."

I knew that my work in this life was not complete. I asked the doctor to fix my heart.

I spent several days at the hospital. My heart valve had been failing long enough that my body had gained twenty-two pounds of fluid. God saved my life. If my daughter had brought me an ex-lax, I would have gone to bed and died.

The doctors sent me home, taking six different medicines. My cousin told me that one of those medicines, Warfarin, was basically rat poison. He said that I would need to take it for the rest of my life. I just do not believe in long-term medicines. Especially not rat poison. On my first and only visit to see my heart surgeon, I asked him about that. He said that would depend on my six-month examination. If everything checked-out in six months, it would be possible to stop taking warfarin.

In six months, I felt great. I said, "Father, is it alright, with you, to stop taking the warfarin?"

He said, "Yes." So I quit taking that medicine.

I had to see my regular doctor in order to get my other prescriptions refilled. A few months after I had stopped the Warfarin, I needed to see him about the other refills.

When he listened to my heart, he said, "What have you done? Your heart is now in AFIB; it is no longer beating in rhythm."

He said that another specialist would stop my heart. Then he would shock my heart to restart it back into rhythm.

I asked God about that, and he said to go.

That specialist set up another hospital appointment for me. Before they could do the restart, they needed to run another scope down into my heart. They needed to find out if any blood clots had formed.

When I woke up, he told me that there were two clots in my heart. He said that one of them was the biggest clot he had ever seen. They put me back on Warfarin for over a year. We did the same procedure again.

When I woke up, he told me that there had been no change in the clots. I went back to my regular doctor. He said that we needed to try a change from the Warfarin. We should try another drug. There was a choice he had, between two drugs. I asked him to pray about it, and he chose Xarelto. I discountinued the drug during the Summer 2017.

The last five years, until the spring of 2017, have mostly been about enduring and obedience. About 3 ½ years have been spent in my chair. God has gotten me out every Friday, except hospital time. On Fridays, I take care of business and buy groceries. Sometimes for several weeks in a row, that would be the schedule that God would have me on.

Early this spring, 2017, the Lord had taken me outside. It was a beautiful day, and I sat down to talk to the Father.

I said, "Father, I think that I understand what Tom was trying to explain to me all those years ago about love. Ev-

THE BOOK OF JOB • 61

erything that you do is love. I do not need to understand all the things that have happened to my family and me. I understand that there is a purpose for every single thing that you have allowed to happen. I would not change one thing. I asked you to use me. I am a soldier in your army."

After that day, the Lord began to share with me, the purpose of my life. Through the years, I had thought about Job many times. God would always say, "That book is more important than you know." All that I knew was, that my life had been crushed like Job's life had been. God asked me about standing in the hedge for Him. I did not understand until He had explained it to me, that Job had done the same thing for the land of Uz.

During the summer of 2017, he began to show me about the legal case that is between Him and Satan.

I know with the writing of this book, that the season in my chair is just about over. What I do not know is my own outcome. I know that God loves me. I also know that Satan was in a very powerful bargaining position. I know that Dr. Arnold Murray, who was the loudest voice against "false rapture" has died. I know that Tom, my mentor, died this summer. God told me, after I started this book, that Tom's death had been demanded by Satan. Satan thought that the death of my mentor might break my foundation.

My doctor had been letting me get refills for my medicines, without giving me a physical exam. The summer of 2017, he refused to do that any longer. I was taking four different prescriptions. They were for my heart and one for my prostate. God said to throw the empty bottles into the garbage, as each one ran out. I knew that there would be a bridge for me to cross at some point in time.

October 2017, I left the apartment needing to accomplish three things. I needed to recycle my garbage, go to town and mail a letter, and get a document copied. I went to the recycle center and delivered the garbage.

I was driving toward Franklin when an attack hit me. My speech was slurred, I had a hard time talking. I said, "Father, do you want me to pull over?" I opened my mouth and said, "Noooo." I knew that I needed to complete what I had started out to do. I got to the post office. My legs had stopped working properly. My left arm had no function. I went down on the ground before I got to the front door. A stranger came by and gave me back the letter that I had dropped. I sat there for several minutes. I managed to get inside and mail the letter. I made it to the copy business and managed to get my work there done. I was weak the next day. I was much better the day after that. I know that what happened to me were the "symptoms" of a stroke. God told me to make out my last will and to let my sister hold it. I have done that.

About two weeks ago, God talked to me about what I would have needed to do, for Satan to win. My test had centered around what God has shown me about "the love and the law." With all the things that have happened to my family and with people that I love, not one time did I get on my knees and ask him to fix anything. I have waited for his love to make things right.

God has not told me about the outcome of my life. I am a winner either way. In June 2017, the Lord wanted me to visit Eagle Mountain International Church (EMIC). An awesome man named Billy Burke was there. They had an event called "Miracles on the Mountain." It lasted for four days. Hundreds of miracles happened during my four-day visit. I believe in miracles. If I live long enough for Brother Copeland to pray for me, then I will be healthy for the next 25 years at least.

If God takes me home, then hallelujah. I will have perfectly fulfilled my destiny. The best times are in front of me. There is no blame or fault to put it on anyone. Either way, I will get to sleep on clean sheets shortly.

When I was about ten years old, I had the same bad dream several nights in a row. There was a big white house sitting out in the middle of an open field. It was a nice house, but it was open, as it was abandoned. I went into the house and walked straight through. Every room was clean but empty. I would go on to the next room. I was in the middle of the house, maybe ten rooms deep. I would get to the center of the house, all the doors in the house would shut. Every room was suddenly full of poison snakes. I would kick and fight to get out of one room only to have the next room be the same way. All those snakes biting at me, room after room. I would always wake up before I got all the way out. I told my mother, she said it was just a bad dream. The dream came back, and Mama found a small Bible. She put the Bible under my pillow and the dream stopped. That dream came back every five or 10 years.

When I started this walk, I asked God about that dream. He said that dream was for a time in front of me. In 2016, God said he wanted me to get back to the gym. I was happy to be able to workout with weights again. I joined a local gym. I had gone to work out about a dozen times.

I was really pleased with the progress that I had made. I started and ended each work out with a ride on the stationary bike. I would work all the machines in the middle. I finished my workout one day. I had just finished wiping-off my perspiration from the bike. I was standing beside the bike when my legs just turned into rubber. I was completely helpless. I leaned against the machine to keep from falling. I remained there for at least 10 minutes. I finally got enough strength back, to make it to one of the chairs beside the front desk. I sat in that chair for at least ten more minutes. Everything turned a deep, golden yellow. I remembered that exact color from a previous spiritual attack. I knew not to speak.

There were at least 20 people there along with the owner. I was amazed that no one had noticed how much trouble I was in. After 10 or 15 minutes I had the strength to make it out to my truck. No sooner had I gotten into my truck, I had one of those terrible diarrhea pains. I just made it back to the apartment in time to avoid a mess. After I came out of the bathroom, I laid down and took a short nap.

When I woke up, I said, "Father, will you tell me what that was all about?"

He said, "That was your dream about the house full of snakes. If you had asked any person for help, you would not have lived."

I have not been back to my doctor since 2016.

Facts & Observations

1. God put Mr. Trump into the White House and surrounded him with a fantastic team of preachers and prophets.
2. Mr. Trump does a great job of giving the glory and praise to God.
3. The millennium is almost here. God will choose the president after Mr. Trump.
4. A man who lives in Nashville, Tennessee, has been told by God, that he will follow Mr. Trump as the next president. His name is Gary Davis. His wife's name is Jay. She is a powerhouse for the Lord. God will show you, Mr. Trump, when it is the proper time to bring Gary Davis into your administration. The experience with you will help him to have a smooth transition.
5. Mr. Trump, Satan hates you. Besides FOX News, the rest of the media hate you. Satan hates you. Hollywood hates you.
6. Mr. Trump, you are the man that God has chosen to wreck the foundations of what Satan has built.
7. Mr. Trump, God has shown me that Satan will attack you as well. In Daniel 4:30, Nebuchadnezzar, King of Babylon, took all the credit and glory for what had been

accomplished in his kingdom. He was removed before the words had left his mouth. Daniel 4:31.

8. Mr. Trump, give God all the credit, and you will be remembered forever.

REMEMBER BRAINPOWER

Men = 1

Satan = 1,000,000

God = 1,000,000,000,000,000,000,000,000,000,000

Mr. Obama

What a hero you could've been! You chose to take the wrong path. Fox News showed your pastor in Chicago. He was screaming at the top of his voice, "God Damn America!" He repeated that same thing. You, Mr. Obama, will stand in front of the God one day. You had your government agencies attack Christians and conservative groups. You declared in the middle of your second term that America was no longer a Christian nation.

You went on national television before the election. You said that none of the officials at the voting centers should check identification. You were pleading for the illegal population to vote. You knew that they would be 100% for Hillary.

You are a bad man. You are a bad person. You will be forgotten.

Mrs. Clinton

Satan had things set up perfectly for this to be the time of judgment. The Sunday morning after the presidential election, I sat down in my chair.

God said, "Do you remember the gas lines back in the 70s?"

I said, "Yes sir, I do."

He said, "What do you remember?"

I said that I remember being able to buy gasoline two times a week. There was a 10 gallon per purchase limit. I remember that the government told us that America had enough gas to last 15 years. They needed to make the gas-that we had last long enough to develop other sources of energy. America sat in those gas lines for months. America said, money no longer matters. I will pay whatever it costs, just give me the gas I want. Wow! All of a sudden there was gas. What we are told was a fifteen year supply has lasted for more than forty years. Now forty years later, we learned that we have a surplus. We have also learned that we have an amazing reserve."

God gave Satan the whole world in their "contract." That includes America.

Our government colluded with the oil companies. They force us to pay more money for gasoline without having a revolt. Europe was paying much higher prices for its gas, which had to be imported.

America has its own oil!

God then asked me if I remembered the national deficit adds that the Democrats had run on television for the Obama campaign. I answered, "Yes sir, I do." I remember that the ad said that we had a national deficit of nine trillion dollars. They said that it had to be brought under control. They said that a $20 trillion dollar deficit was America's drop dead broke number. They said that America could not possibly recover from a deficit of $20 trillion dollars. God said that if Mrs. Clinton had won the election that the deficit would have grown to as much as $25-$30 trillion dollars. Satan would have finished destroying America's will to work. Mrs. Clinton would have called a press conference. She would've told America that it was officially broke. Her administration had fought a valiant fight. America had been told more than ten years ago, about that drop-dead broke number. However, there was a light at the end of the tunnel. The world leaders have gotten together. They come up with a plan that would work.

There would now be a new one world government. There would now be only one world currency. This would have resulted in God's judgment coming now.

Secret Societies

Satan is the source of lies and secrets. There was a point in my life that I had become a prosperous businessman. A man who is a friend of mine invited me to a party that was being put on by the Freemasons. The food was great. The men were the business leaders of our town. These men all have very good reputations. I knew several of those men. I had respect for them, and I liked them. I felt that an invitation to join them would have been an honor. They embrace God and do work to honor him. That is just how sneaky Satan can be. The top national layers of this secret society belong to Satan. Mr. Thomas Horn, a man on television, had a lot of information to share about these people. He said that 43 of our founding fathers were Freemasons. That sounded great. He said that the Freemasons had designed the layout for our nation's capitol, Washington DC. He had aerial photos that reveal that our capitol is laid out on the basis of 666. That is Satan's number. The capitol building is where all of our presidents are inaugurated. The capitol building was designed by the Freemasons. Mr. Horn had a picture looking up into the dome of the building. Looking up into the dome is a huge mural depicting heaven.

Neither God nor Jesus is there. Several of the beings pictured there have horns. Below heaven in the ceiling are a ring of statues. Currently there are one hundred statues as each state in the union can contribute two.

Satan has America tied up in a web of deception and lies that is amazing. There are two secret societies that control all of the money, and thus the world. About seven years ago, a friend at church; gave me a DVD and asked me to watch it. The name of the DVD was the Obama deception. The content was not at all like the name sounded. There was a man standing in front of the Bilderberg office in Virginia. The man pointed at their office and said, "These are the people that run the world." He said that America's middle-class people had gotten control of too much money. He said that they had created the housing bubble which burst between 2007 and 2009.

He said that one day, in 1913, that 13 members of Congress showed up to work one day. That day, with only 13 members present, they voted in the Federal Reserve System. They gave America's money to a private group of people.

He said that no president since Kennedy had been elected without them. He said that they might have been responsible for the assassination of President Lincoln. He said that during Mr. Obama's campaign, there was a time that he was scheduled to be in Kansas City. He instead had gone back to Virginia to meet with the Bilderberg group. His campaign manager told the crowd that he was needed in another place and could not be there.

Political Facts: Satan Wants America Broke

Shame on you John Lewis, Maxine Waters, and you older members of the Black Caucus. Shame on you, Rev. Al Sharpton, and you religious leaders, who know the truth. You have all become rich and powerful by spreading Satan's hate across America. You all know that after Lyndon Johnson became president he sent out 100,000 social workers. He sent them through the cities of America to destroy your race. The social workers told the black women to have babies and get rid of their husbands. Money from each additional child would raise their income level from the government. That is the basis for the term "welfare Cadillac." The formula was simple: more children; no husband. The government check would pay for a better lifestyle. Once you have enough children, you can have a new Cadillac. It was bribery, but it worked. Tens of thousands of Cadillacs were sold to single black women. Satan used the Democratic Party to destroy the morality of the black people. 70% of black children today have no legal father. Between 85 and 90% of the black people today vote Democrat.

My heart has always been with the class of Americans who want to work and be productive. I am a Republican, but I would've changed to the Democratic Party. By the time I was old enough to vote, I clearly heard Democrats preaching hate. Those rich Republicans hate you.

God does not hate.

Every human being deserves to be loved by another human being. There is a major problem with same-sex relationships. They cannot bear children. God created us to bear him children.

Satan embraced the Democratic Party. The democrat platform has embraced Satan's policies. They believe in human rights, abortion, and same-sex marriage. God is never going to fix the Democratic Party and put it back in control. Millions of Democrats are wonderful people of faith. If you are registered as a Democrat, it is likely the party of your mother and father. LBJ destroyed your party. You need to walk away.

The Republican platform has embraced God as its main focus. God has embraced the Republican Party.

The KKK and other hate groups are not welcome in the Republican Party.

Satan owns and controls the "swamp" in Washington. Mr. Trump is going to drain the "swamp." Many people have left his administration and Congress. Others will follow shortly. Republicans will be gone as well as the Democrats.

Vote Christian.

False Friends

Satan is very serious. During Mr. Obama's presidency, our deficit went from $9 trillion to almost 20,000,000,000,000. During his presidency Mr. Obama created confusion. Money was going in so many directions that no one could keep track of it all. One news agency reported that they had tried to track all the money down. The record showed at least 3 trillion dollars that could not be found at all. The goal of Satan and the secret groups is a one world government and a one world currency. Money does not just disappear. These groups have unlimited money and power. They control many members in both houses of Congress. They control most of the media. About two months ago, there were three men of God on one of the Christian channels. Mr. Thomas Horn was one of those men. He said that last year, Mr. Mitch McConnell, leader of the Republican Senate, and Mr. Paul Ryan, leader of Republican House; had gone to meet with the Bilderberg Group. The Bilderberg Group does not control Mr. Trump. Mr. Trump wanted to do taxes first. Those two men assured Mr. Trump that the best way to go forward was to pass their health care plan first. They wanted Mr. Trump to believe that healthcare was the key to getting the tax bill passed.

Trump is the first president in many years that the Bilderberg Group does not control. The Bilderberg Group want to control Mr. Trump, until the next election. Mr. Ryan and Mr. McConnell had nothing that even resembled a healthcare plan. Mr. Trump assured the American people that the

Republicans had a "beautiful" healthcare plan to give the American people. Taxes should have been done first. These two men, together, have brought a great plan by Mr. Trump to a grinding halt. Mr. McConnell said, "I believe that Mr. Trump has excessive expectations."

Satan is a Hillary Clinton supporter. Our "deep state" is at least 85% Clinton voters. Satan can talk a very smart people into doing some very dumb things. There are people in the sixteen government agencies who have worked very hard to have Mr. Trump impeached. They are experts at what they do. They have tried to make what they have done look like it was the Russians.

Mr. Trump is a man of God. Mr. Trump said that he was going to drain the "swamp" when he got to Washington. Mr. Trump did not understand just how "deep" that swamp truly is.

There is a *really* bright light at the end of this tunnel.

To The President:

Mr. Trump, Satan Wants America to Go Broke

What Satan used to try to stall your accomplishments, God would see you turn to your benefit. Healthcare: as long as Americans have the freedom and access to smoking and alcohol, there is no good solution. Smoking destroys your lungs and eventually kills you. Alcohol destroys your liver and kidneys. It is not right for Americans that do not have those two problems to pay for the ones that do. Those two groups of people are free will, self-inflicted medical disasters. The millennium will fix these types of problems. Prop up the current system for a short time. God will fix this healthcare problem during your presidency.

The law that mandates employers to provide medical insurance needs to be repealed. This is how it works in reality: huge corporations, like Walmart, are forced to hire the majority of their labor as part-time help. 29 hours a week spread out over several days. This erratic work schedule leaves the worker with about 300 dollars per week. It forces them to buy Obama care and seek a second job. Those workers struggle to make ends meet financially. It would be much better to let those millions of people have a full-time job. Corporations would again have to compete for the best people. Job security and peace of mind.

The Climate

I was watching a nature program on television. There have been about 1500 volcanoes on the earth. There are about six hundred active volcanoes, on the earth now. I went to sleep and had a dream. In the dream, there was a large temperature gauge, hanging on the wall. When I woke up, I asked God to explain the dream. He said that the volcanoes belong to him and that He controls the temperature of the earth. "Those volcanoes are burning fossil fuel." He put that fuel in the ground for a purpose. He put that fuel there for man to use.

Exploring cost-efficient ways to use the sun and the wind are very good ideas. For Americans to spend money sending scientists to measure the melting of glaciers and blame that loss on humans is stupid. These are the same people who have explained to us stupid people that we are evolved from monkeys. That theory needs to be taken out of our schools.

Israel

Mr. Trump, God recently kept you from making a huge mistake. He gave you the unction to recognize Jerusalem as the true capitol of Israel. The Palestinians then rejected the U.S. as a negotiator. The U.S. must have NO part in negotiating any split of Jerusalem or Israel. The spiritual world controls this world. God has told His prophets that if your administration takes part in dividing Israel, that He would divide the United States.

There is a fault line that lies at the western end of Tennessee, the New Madrid Seismic Zone. Two of these prophets has been on Jim Bakker's Christian program. A prophet named Sadhu Sundar Selvaraj, said this fault would open up. An Austrian Jew, saved by Jesus himself from being killed as a child, has the second part of that prophecy. She had the vision in the 1980's where she saw the Great Lakes draining into the Gulf of Mexico.

God will settle the division problem with Israel Himself. Let Him.

Available Programs

I was broke for a while. One of my daughter's needed help financially. I was unable to meet her needs, but I took her to the local social service office to apply for food stamps. The office was full. There was not a black woman in there. There was not another white woman in there.

The biggest source of income for the country of Mexico is the $22 billion sent home by Mexicans who are working in America.

When I had my grading business, I am employed 10 to 12 Mexican workers, full-time. They each had two forms of identification. They were great workers. They were smart. They were a joy to be around. My grading company failed. Before it failed, I was talking with the man that led the Mexican crew. I asked the man how many of our men are legal.

He said not one! There are lots of people who need the help that this workforce provides. I paid all my Mexican workers from $10-$12 per hour. That was almost ten years ago. I respected them, and I needed them.

The men work. The women take their children to our government to get all the aid that they can apply for.

Mr. President, it is wrong for Americans to buy each of these people $500 each month in food stamps. Tell these folks that if they sign their name on the government form to get aid, that you will deport them. They are no better than we are. They are sending $22 billion a year home, and we are feeding them. If your job doesn't support your family, go home.

Revelation 2:27 says, "And he shall rule them with a rod of iron; as the vessels of a potter shall they be broken to shivers."

Mr. President, God, has chosen you to be this man. That verse is the description of your job.

Big Pharma

They have thrown billions of dollars at our Congress. They have colluded with the doctors and lawmakers to keep their crimes legal. They have addicted and killed millions of people, for profit.

I had open heart surgery three years ago. I had six prescriptions when I left the hospital. I sent $200 with my daughter to get those filled. Mission Hospital, in Asheville, North Carolina, did the surgery. I was taken downstairs to be released. My daughter went to get my medicine. All six prescriptions cost $127. Those prescriptions were a thirty day supply. I sent my daughter with $200 to the local Walgreens. The doctor had told me to not stop the Warfarin and the Amiodarone. Walgreens gave her the new customer discount. She came home with the Amiodarone only. It had cost 155 dollars.

I was not supposed to drive a vehicle for at least six weeks. I was out of medicine, so I drove to Asheville the next day. I walked into the Mission Hospital pharmacy. They filled the six prescriptions for $127. I asked the pharmacist if he had given me a special price because I had been a patient there. He said no. I asked what the Amiodarone had cost. He replied 15 dollars and fifty-five cents. I asked, "Are you making money at your prices?" He said, "Yes, you cannot stay in business without making a profit." Walgreens had charged me 1000% more than Mission pharmacy. That was out of my pocket, and it made me mad.

I know that there are millions of people that our government pays for part or all of their drug expenses. It did not take me very long to figure out that it cost our government billions of dollars each month. This amounts to legal fraud. The congressman for this area is Mark Meadows. I called his office and told his secretary exactly what it happened to me. She said Mr. Meadows was busy, but that she would relay this information to him.

That was almost three years ago. There are 3 million people that have applied to the government to pay for their Hepatitis C cure.

It only costs $96,000 per patient. An eight week supply will cure one patient.

Mr. President, forget Congress. Have your lawyers write your bill for you. Make it illegal for congressman and doctors to take one dollar from big Pharma. Go to the American people. Tell the congressmen that if they do not pass this, that you are going to publish every name that votes against you. This bill should be passed in 120 days or less.

Selling out your country is nothing short of treason. Jail time should be mandatory for those congressmen who do not want to help expose what each guilty man has done.

Jail time for the executives of big Pharma should happen. Collusion with our lawmakers is a crime.

CHAPTER EIGHT

Prayers That Will Work For You

I have never heard a preacher tell about how to build a great relationship with God, other than read your Bible and pray.

This is what the Lord said to tell you. Define your prayer closet. That needs to be a place that is without distraction. Prayer is simply talking to God. Tell God that you are there to seek Him, with all your heart. It is a sin to covet what belongs to someone else. However, it is just as big a sin, to not take what God wants to give you.

> "Verily I say unto you, whatsoever ye shall bind on earth shall be bound in heaven: and what so ever you shall loose on earth shall be loosed in heaven." - Matthew 18:18

This entirely reflects our relationship with Jesus. The Lord had me pray this prayer.

"Father, anything that you want me to have, both here on earth and in heaven, I want it all, missing nothing. Father, I asked that you build a relationship with me that yokes me with things that you would like to give me."

Give God 20 minutes a day, every day, for the rest of your life. The first 10 minutes, thank God for everything that comes to your mind since the last time you prayed. For the second 10 minutes, close your eyes and look at the back of your eyelids. It takes some practice, but shut off all thought.

Create silence; we are too loud. Thoughts will try to come, shut them off. Yes, it is meditation. Train yourself to go the whole 10 minutes without having thought. You will know when a thought comes that is from the Lord. When they come, and they will come, talk to him about that thought. God said that if anyone would faithfully give him this 20 minutes a day, within one year, they would need an hour.

You need to read at least one chapter per day in your Bible. It is medicine for your soul. When I tell anyone about this, God always has me say: "Your whole future is in your own hands."

This method will work for anyone of any age, color, or nationality, without discrimination. We are a people who strive to avoid commitment and responsibility. We want to say "well, God knows my heart." That is not the way that God works. He expects every person to open your mouth and say, "I'm all in Father, use me." Without being "all in," you are just playing games.

> *"Humble yourselves therefore under the mighty hand of God, that He may exalt you in due time." - 1 Peter 5:6*

Time does not mean much to God, as it is endless with Him. He will use time to test you, but He will always be there for you in time.

CHAPTER NINE

The Wedding

This book is awesome news. It is the "time" for our churches to turn around and go against Satan.

Just after the Summer Olympics, in 2016, I had a dream. The dream was a side view of the team of rowers, rowing their boat. It was beautiful to see. Each arm was strong and pulling perfectly in unison.

When I woke up, I said, "Father, what was I looking at?"

He replied, "That is your family. I will bring them back together. When they come out of my fire, they will be a tremendous prayer team for me."

I said, "Hallelujah, I like that a lot."

Two nights later, I had another dream. In this dream, I could look down at myself, lying below me. I pulled a cover-up on me, and on that cover were the Olympic rings.

When I woke up, I said to the Father, "That is the second time in three days that I have had a dream that had the Olympics in it. What does that mean?"

He replied, "The thing that I will be talking to you about will happen before the next Summer Olympics."

In 1948, Israel was declared a nation by the UN. The parable of the fig tree says that this generation will not pass away before the Scriptures are fulfilled. Seventy years from 1948 is 2018. Jesus said let no man will know the day or hour of his coming.

> "Surely the Lord God will do nothing, but He revealeth His secret to His servants, the prophets." - Amos 3:7

Summer of 2017, the Lord said, "What I am talking to you about is the millennium. Before the next Summer Olympics, Jesus will say, 'My family is finished.' At that second, grace has ended and the millennium will be here. That is the "dividing of times.'"

All those wonderful promises that are in the Bible are about to take place. People need to understand that there are simply not enough Christians to take over the world right now. God said that he would do this gradually. He said that within 25 years from the beginning of the millennium that the world would be completely changed. That by then you would either be a child of God, or you would be working for someone who was. Satan will be in hell. There will be no sin. God has chosen one man to lead the world. Every world leader will be a Christian.

The Lord said, "Within 28 years from now, battleships will be melted down for the steel to be used in buildings and bridges."

All the things that we have to waste our money on, such as crime, will be gone. America will lead the world and be rich for it.

Right now, Satan owns the Law and the world. Many sick, poor people love God. He said that what a person owns during the millennium will be a direct reflection of that person's relationship with Him.

CHAPTER TEN

The Church and The Prophets

There are a thousand years of peace between here and the judgment. At that time, the false prophets will call for continued peace. The second strongest statement that God has spoken to me is: "I have told no man on the face of the earth that he is going anywhere." Churches, it is time to attack Satan.

> "And if the prophet be deceived when he hath spoken a thing, I the LORD have deceived that prophet, and I will stretch out my hand upon him, and will destroy him from the midst of my people Israel." - Ezekiel 14:9

There are many wonderful prophets in the world today. There are many preachers and millions of people who look to you for guidance. Let go of Gog and Magog. God is clearly shaking his people. There are more things coming that God will talk to you about.

PREACHERS

God is not mad at any of you right now. You're preaching rapture now was in His contract with Satan. The understanding of this book is the end of God's saints; preaching Satan's message.

Repent simply means to change. Repent now and preach boldly against Satan. You are God's saints. Make a "big deal" every Sunday about the shrinking time that Satan has left here now. Satan will go to hell exposed with no glory left at all. Dedicate the songs of your choir to the demise of that old beast. Preach on the Bible promises of health and prosperity. Make your church a miserable place for Satan to be. He will leave you alone. Your church will experience miracles and revival, as it has never known.

Before the next Summer Olympics is the time frame. God will close the door and have His wedding.

> "A good man leaveth an inheritance to his children's children: and wealth of the sinner is laid up for the just." - Proverbs 13:22

Within 25 years, the wealth of the world will be transferred to his bride.

This is the time of great revival before the harvest. The churches that preach these messages will fill up and flow over.

> "But this will be the covenant that I will make with the house of Israel; after those days, saith the Lord, I will put my law in their inward parts, and write it in their hearts; and will be their God, and they shall be

my people. And they shall teach no more every man his neighbor, and every man his brother, saying know the Lord: for they shall all know me, from the least of them unto the greatest of them, saith the Lord: for I will forgive their iniquity, and I will remember their sin no more." - Jeremiah 31:33-34

We are in the last days of grace. It is the end of Satan owning the world. Every single person will go to church. "After those days" refers to right now. This is the time of grace. The door will close on these days, and Jesus will have his wedding. "I will put my law in their inward parts, and write it in their heart." That verse is perfectly clear. Grace is going. Satan is down. God's family will have formed itself. People only want to do what is right in God's eyes. Preaching in the churches will come to an end. No one will commit crimes. No one will sin.

Saturday and Sunday will be the Sabbath. Musicians and singers will serve in the church. There will be two full days of singing and praising the Lord. There will be 1000 years of love and harmony in the world.

The Millenium Church and Our Leader

God always saves His best for the last. There've been many great men of God. There are many today. Only the very best is worthy to lead God's church into the millennium.

> *"And he that overcometh and keepeth my works unto the end, to him will I give power over the nations: 27 And he shall rule them with a rod of iron; as the vessels of a potter shall they be broken shivers: even as I received of my Father. 28 And I will give him the morning star." - Revelation 2:26-28*

In the 1970s, God told brother Kenneth Copeland, to build Him a church. He helped Kenneth to acquire a large piece of land to build the church on. God told brother Kenneth that his church would be the revival capitol of the world. Brother Copeland named God's church, Eagle Mountain International Church. This church is God's millennium Church. Brother Kenneth Copeland is the man that God has chosen to lead the world into the millennium.

Brother Copeland will oversee the entire transformation of the whole world. He will live long enough to see it all happen. He will name every nation's leader after the millennium starts. God will work with Brother Copeland to understand lies that bind each denomination.

Each denomination will be prayed for individually. The Christian church will be set free. Big chunks of glory will be stripped from Satan every time a church is set free.

God will turn Brother Copeland's focus to other religions after he is finished with the Christian church. Satan will go into hell completely stripped of his former glory.

I had two visions about this. In the first vision, the world was a large Christmas tree. The top of the tree was bright, but I could still look at it. There were lots of other lights on the tree, but less bright than the top. The top light grew so bright that I could no longer look at it. Lights around the tree started to do the same thing. The whole tree turned on. The tree was so bright that I could no longer look at it.

The second vision is this. I saw the whole world as a human body. Brother Copeland was the head. Pastor George; his wife Terry, and the EMIC Ministry was the neck. Countless thousands of small heads formed the rest of the body. The vision ended. I said, "Father, would you explain that to me?" God said, "Can the body understand before the head does?"

I ask Brother Copeland to pray for my family and me. God said that when Brother Copeland prays for my family, he will put his hedge of protection back around us.

Brother Copeland, God said for you to say: "Father, you have a prayer for Van Rogers and his family." Then just say, "Father –" as He will supply the rest of the words.

CHAPTER ELEVEN

Love

The strongest statement that God made to me is, "I take the blame for nothing; I take the credit for absolutely everything."

I spent a lot of time trying to understand the depth of that statement.

"I have yet many things to say unto you, but ye cannot bear them now." - John 16:12

Jesus would have needed to explain the whole two thousand years to them. They would have needed to know about the millennium and the completion of His family to understand free will.

It is too early to stop looking at any situation until you have seen the victory of God's love in it.

"And we know that all things work together for good to them that love God, to them who are called according to his purpose." - Romans 8:28

God has defeated every situation, bar none.

There are hundreds of levels in God's family. Hitler will not be treated like Billy Graham. When Peter was talking about our trials, in 1 Peter 1:6, he uses three words together: "if need be." We defy God, and he brings things to happen, for our benefit. Every single thing that either God or that Satan does to you, will benefit you in some way. God's love will simply not allow defeat.

We live for such a short time. Eternity is endless. God says that He would rather us be hot or cold, not lukewarm. (Revelation 3:16)

We can be too tall, too short, beautiful, ugly, rich, famous, powerful, neglected or badly bruised. That list goes on and on. Being poor or ugly can be just as bad for you spiritually is being rich or beautiful. They are all barriers that God knows we can overcome. What good does it do for you to own the world for a few years and then have to mow yards for the rest of eternity? Why be angry over any circumstance it keeps you from the place that God has prepared for you? Satan brings hate; God brings love.

Look at these hurricanes and other tragedies that have happened recently. How many million people that support abortion gave their money, their time, and even their tears, in support of the survivors?

Go all in. God expects us to open our mouth and say, "Father I am all in. Please use me."

> *"For the eyes of the Lord run to and from throughout the whole Earth, to show himself strong on behalf of them whose heart is perfect toward him." - II Chronicles 16:9*

Perfect means "all in." No one can make that commitment for you. Peace and love be unto you. AMEN!

CHAPTER TWELVE

Me Personally

I had thought that I would join one of the large ministries. I thought that it would be fulfilling to work with one of them in this coming great harvest. The Lord has shown me that He might open other doors. My testimony would resonate on college campuses. College students are taught that God is just a theory. Any student that is serious about their future would love to hear true stories about a living, working God. Business school students would love to hear about the God that can move lawyers and wealthy landowners to do his bidding.

Legal-minded businessmen would be impressed with the way that God moved people in my life to do what was legally impossible.

I will go exactly where God wants me to.

The End of Job's Story

It is for me today. It is for each of God's children tomorrow.

The Lord had me to finish His book this way:

The first thirty-two verses in the book of Job explain Job's part in the "contract" between God and Satan. This is about the last chapter. His friends brought fourteen animals that were sacrificed to the Lord. This food would have fed Job for a time. He then received a piece of money and gold earring from every man. In buying this book, you have given me a piece of your money. I will pray on a monthly basis for the people who send me gifts.

> P. Van Rogers
> PO Box 541
> Franklin, NC 28744

The last page of this book will be prepared for you. Sign your name, claiming this book as your own. Your address needs to be put below your name as I have done with my name.

These are directions given by the Lord.
I Love You.
Amen

My Name: _____

My Address:

_____

_____

Van with the girls while they were children.

From the Publisher

"Van came to see me when he had worked through most of his manuscript. He approached me as a friend first but a man with a divine message foremost. Given that I am asked multiple times a day to hear someone's elevator pitch regarding a manuscript they just know I am going to be interested in publishing I am always guarded. I was even more so with Van when he alluded to the religious nature of the manuscript.

I want what I write and what I help others publish to honor God, always. I had never seen such a fight from the enemy to keep this book from being in your hands. I prayed over this project and sought the Holy Spirit's guidance over publishing such a polarizing book. I was told to help Van and that I would be blessed for it. I also had a dream about this project. I was shown that Van was led by the Holy Spirit in writing this book. Take heed to what is written in these pages and question what others have told you. Seek God for yourself while He may be found.

God is always true to His promises. Remember that for your own life. I've seen through publishing this book for Van that I'm blessed indeed as my publishing company is growing more quickly than I ever dreamed possible.

Thank you, Van, for your obedience in writing this book and for letting me be the one to bring this to market."

- Monica Collier, Novelist & Publisher
monicacollier.com
redpressco.com

www.ingramcontent.com/pod-product-compliance
Lightning Source LLC
LaVergne TN
LVHW021538080426
835509LV00019B/2703